CHINESE MYTHOLOGY

Huangdi
Yellow Emperor

BY JEAN KUO LEE

CONTENT CONSULTANT
GANG LIU, PhD
ASSOCIATE TEACHING PROFESSOR
CARNEGIE MELLON UNIVERSITY

Kids Core
An Imprint of Abdo Publishing
abdobooks.com

abdobooks.com

Published by Abdo Publishing, a division of ABDO, PO Box 398166, Minneapolis, Minnesota 55439. Copyright © 2023 by Abdo Consulting Group, Inc. International copyrights reserved in all countries. No part of this book may be reproduced in any form without written permission from the publisher. Kids Core™ is a trademark and logo of Abdo Publishing.

Printed in the United States of America, North Mankato, Minnesota.
102022
012023

THIS BOOK CONTAINS
RECYCLED MATERIALS

Cover Photo: Iberfoto Archivo/SuperStock
Interior Photos: Science History Images/Alamy, 4–5, 12–13; F. Jack Jackson/Alamy, 6; Red Line Editorial, 9; Visual China Group/Getty Images, 10; Shutterstock Images, 14, 16, 26, 28 (top), 28 (bottom); Lintao Zhang/Getty Images News/Getty Images, 18–19; Dong Xuming/Visual China Group/Getty Images, 20, 29 (bottom); Pictures from History/Universal Images Group/Getty Images, 22, 29 (top); Zhang Yuan/China News Service/Getty Images, 24

Editor: Ann Schwab
Series Designer: Ryan Gale

Library of Congress Control Number: 2022940676

Publisher's Cataloging-in-Publication Data

Names: Lee, Jean Kuo, author.
Title: Huangdi: Yellow Emperor / by Jean Kuo Lee
Description: Minneapolis, Minnesota: Abdo Publishing, 2023 | Series: Chinese Mythology | Includes online resources and index.
Identifiers: ISBN 9781532199950 (lib. bdg.) | ISBN 9781098275150 (ebook)
Subjects: LCSH: Deities--Juvenile literature. | Gods, Chinese--Juvenile literature. | Mythology, Chinese--Juvenile literature.
Classification: DDC 299.51--dc23

CONTENTS

CHAPTER 1
The Most Powerful Ruler 4

CHAPTER 2
A Peacemaking Warrior 12

CHAPTER 3
The Ancestor of Chinese People 18

Legendary Facts 28
Glossary 30
Online Resources 31
Learn More 31
Index 32
About the Author 32

Huangdi, *center*, is known as the Yellow Emperor. He is one of the most famous rulers of ancient China.

The Most Powerful Ruler

In the land of mythical China, a Divine Emperor ruled part of the region. His name was Huangdi, or the Yellow Emperor. He was a good ruler. He loved his people.

A stone marker stands at Huangdi's birthplace in Xinzheng, China.

But another emperor, Yandi, ruled the other part of the land. They became enemies. They fought for control. The fierce battles ended when Huangdi finally won. Then the land rested in peace.

Huangdi became a powerful ruler. He unified the country. He ruled China for 100 years.

Huangdi became the first of the Divine Emperors. People in China told stories about them and wrote those stories down. The Divine Emperors became gods.

Taoism

Tao means "the way" in the Chinese language Mandarin. Taoism is a belief system that began in China more than 2,000 years ago. Today, it is a major religion and **philosophy** in China and Taiwan. The Yellow Emperor is a key figure in Taoism.

Powerful Rulers

Chinese myths say that the Five Divine Emperors ruled China a long time ago. Nobody knows whether they were real people. Chinese philosophy teaches that the world is made up of five elements. These elements are wood, fire, metal, water, and earth. Each emperor ruled over one of the elements. The emperors also each had a color. These were green, red, white, black, or yellow.

The Yellow Emperor was named for his color. He ruled over the element of earth. He became a hero to the Chinese people. He is one of the most famous legendary figures in Chinese culture.

The Five Divine Emperors

Zhuanxu

Direction: North

Element: Water

Color: Black

Shaohao

Direction: West

Element: Metal

Color: White

Huangdi

Direction: Center

Element: Earth

Color: Yellow

Taihao

Direction: East

Element: Wood

Color: Green

Yandi

Direction: South

Element: Fire

Color: Red

The Five Divine Emperors hold great meaning for Chinese people. Each emperor has his own color and position and controls an element.

The myths about Huangdi remain popular today.
People continue to share his story and honor him.

What Is Chinese Mythology?

Chinese myths are stories about gods and
goddesses. They explain human nature and

the creation of the universe. The people of China recorded myths in ancient writings. The earliest writings go back to about 3,000 years ago. Chinese people continue to tell the myths today. They sing them as entertainment during weddings and funerals. They share the stories with each other to explain history.

Further Evidence

Look at the website below. Does it give any new evidence to support Chapter One?

The Four-Faced Yellow Emperor of Mythistory

abdocorelibrary.com/huangdi

Huangdi is known as a wise ruler who protected his people.

CHAPTER 2

A Peacemaking Warrior

One night, a bolt of lightning circled a star. The bright light lit up the sky. Mother Fubao became pregnant and gave birth to Huangdi. He grew up to be smart, honest, clever, and wise.

Huangdi was a fierce and clever warrior.

Huangdi did not like war. He only fought others so that he could keep peace. His most famous battles were against Yandi and Chiyou. The Yellow Emperor used nature to fight his wars. He controlled powerful beasts and birds.

He got help from strong animals to attack his enemies. He could stop the rain from falling. Then other armies would die from **drought**.

Another way Huangdi fought was with cleverness. He made a drum from the hide of a mythical creature. The drum was so loud it stopped the enemy from escaping. He also blew horns that sounded like dragons to scare his enemies.

Who Were Yandi and Chiyou?

Yandi was also called the Flame Emperor. Chiyou was another well-known leader. Some people believe *Flame Emperor* was a title given to a number of leaders. They think that Chiyou might have been one of these leaders too.

Some stories say that a dragon took Huangdi to heaven after he died.

Mighty Warrior

Some say Huangdi fought as many as 55 wars.

There are many versions of myths about

Huangdi. Some say he became **immortal**.

Others say he chose the date of his death.

In one ancient text, a historian describes the Yellow Emperor:

> *Born a genius he could speak when a baby, as a boy he was quick and smart, as a youth simple and earnest, and when grown up intelligent.*

Source: Sima Qian. "Shiji: Records of the Grand Historian: Annals of the Five Emperors." *Chinese Text Project*, n.d., ctext.org. Accessed 18 Mar. 2022.

What's the Big Idea?

Read the primary source text carefully. What is the main idea? Explain how the main idea is supported by details.

Today, Chinese people honor Huangdi for his contributions to their country.

CHAPTER 3

The Ancestor of Chinese People

Today, Han Chinese people see themselves as descendants of the Yellow Emperor. As a legendary leader, the Yellow Emperor ruled the people who later became the Huaxia ethnic group.

The Han Chinese people celebrate the Yellow Emperor as their ancestor.

Their descendants, the Han Chinese people, believe that the Yellow Emperor is their ancient **ancestor**. Non-Han ethnic groups such as Mongolians also see the Yellow Emperor as their ancestor. Today, he is a symbol of unity for 56 different ethnic groups in China. Having one common ancestor unites these groups and gives them a shared **identity**.

Founder of Chinese Culture and Civilization

The Yellow Emperor cut trees and used the wood for fire and shelter. He made boats and carts. He invented types of hats and clothes.

Cangjie, an official of the Yellow Emperor, is known as the inventor of Chinese language writing characters. According to the myths, he had four eyes.

He tamed horses and cattle so they could do work. Coins were invented with his help. He asked his officials to study the sun, moon, and stars. Music, writing, and math all began with his reign. He started rituals and developed Chinese medicine. His wife, Leizu, was the first to use thread from silkworms to make silk fabric.

There are more stories of how the Yellow Emperor created Chinese culture and civilization. These myths are thousands of years old. They are still told in China today.

The Invention of Writing

According to legend, an official of the Yellow Emperor invented the first Chinese language writing **characters**. On the night that the characters were created, it is said that the demons and ghosts cried because they could no longer cheat humans.

People gather at the Yellow Emperor's mausoleum to pay tribute to him.

Memorials to the Yellow Emperor

Chinese people worship the Yellow Emperor as their ancestor. His **mausoleum** was built at least 2,000 years ago on Mount Qiao. It is called the First Mausoleum of China. Some stories say Huangdi's body was taken to heaven when he died, so all that is buried there is his clothing.

The site covers an area of 1.5 square miles (4 square kilometers). There are more than 8,000 cypress trees growing there. Many of these trees are more than 1,000 years old. Stories say that Huangdi planted one of the trees.

Giant statues of the heads of Huangdi, *right*, and Yandi have been carved from a mountain. They are both considered ancestors of the Chinese people.

Emperors from the past honored Huangdi by placing stone slabs describing their sacrifices to him. People continue to offer sacrifices at his temple. It is on the same site as the mausoleum. They burn incense and pray.

In 2007, huge new statues of Huangdi and Yandi were created. Their faces are carved on the side of a mountain in central China. People continue to respect and honor the Yellow Emperor today.

LEGENDARY FACTS

The Yellow Emperor became powerful by defeating other warriors.

Stories say Huangdi rode a dragon to heaven after he died.

Chinese writing, medicine, and arithmetic are said to have been invented under the Yellow Emperor's rule.

The Chinese people, both Han and non-Han groups, see the Yellow Emperor as their common ancestor.

Glossary

ancestor
a person who lived long ago from whom more recent family members descended

characters
pictures that represent words

drought
a long period of dry weather without rain

identity
features or beliefs that make a person or group of people unique

immortal
living forever

mausoleum
a large building that houses a tomb

philosophy
the most basic beliefs, concepts, and attitudes of an individual or group

Online Resources

To learn more about Huangdi and Chinese mythology, visit our free resource websites below.

Visit **abdocorelibrary.com** or scan this QR code for free Common Core resources for teachers and students, including vetted activities, multimedia, and booklinks, for deeper subject comprehension.

Visit **abdobooklinks.com** or scan this QR code for free additional online weblinks for further learning. These links are routinely monitored and updated to provide the most current information available.

Learn More

Avrick, Rachel. *Chinese Character Practice Workbook for Kids*. Rockridge, 2021.

Hamby, Zachary. *Introduction to Mythology for Kids*. Rockridge, 2020.

Index

Chinese language writing
  characters, 23
Chiyou, 14–15

Divine Emperor, 5, 7–9

ethnic groups, 21

First Mausoleum of China,
  25, 27
five elements, 8–9
Flame Emperor, 15

Han Chinese people, 19, 21
Huaxia ethnic group, 19

Leizu, 23

Mongolians, 21
Mount Qiao, 25

Taoism, 7

Yandi, 6, 9, 14–15, 27

About the Author

Jean Kuo Lee is a Chinese American writer. She writes fiction and nonfiction books for curious kids.